Harriet Quimby

America's First Lady of the Air

A Biography for Intermediate Readers

ANITA P. DAVIS
AND
ED. Y. HALL

Published by
THE HONORIBUS PRESS
POST OFFICE BOX 4872
SPARTANBURG , SC 29305

An HONORIBUS PRESS
AVIATION HISTORY SERIES BOOK

First Printing April 1998

ISBN: 1-885354-06-1

Printed in the United States of America.

PROLOGUE

A RESCUE ATTEMPT

Harriet Quimby was terrified! Her passenger William Willard was standing in the open cockpit. He had unhooked his safety harness while Harriet was busy piloting the Bleriot monoplane. His movements were placing them both in jeopardy.

Even in 1912 the woman pilot Harriet understood the principles of flight and quickly realized the dangers to her passenger and to herself. As William Willard moved about in the rear of the Bleriot monoplane, his weight upset the delicate balance of the aircraft. The forward motion of the airplane and the fast-moving air made it difficult for him to stand without falling forward. Gravity, too, was trying to claim its prize.

Harriet was a fanatic on aircraft safety. Three American women had already died in flight. Harriet had made sure that William Willard was secure before they began the pleasure ride across Dorchester Bay to Boston Lighthouse and back. She herself double-checked her own safety harness. She would not dream of leaving the ground in an open airplane without being secured in her seat.

(Courtesy Branch County Library, Cold Water, Michigan)

A Bleriot XI, the type flown by Harriet Quimby during her short flying career.

Despite these precautions, something had gone wrong. The motion of the airplane had caused nausea in the inexperienced passenger. William had unhooked his safety harness. He had wanted to vomit over the side of the airplane so he would not soil his clothes and the seat of the airplane. He had tried to stand in the open airplane and to tell Harriet of his problem.

Harriet knew the danger that William faced in the upright position. She tried to tell him to sit down, but he persisted in leaning over her seat and trying to talk above the noise of the engine.

Again Harriet screamed from the front seat of the open cockpit for Mr. Willard to get back in his seat and to fasten his safety harness. Her voice sounded weak against the engine's roar.

Things were becoming more serious. William Willard was falling against Harriet, the pilot! She shouted against the wind and the noise of the engine for him to sit down, but he seemed not to hear.

Next she tried to push Mr. Willard back into his rear seat, but she could not move freely with her safety harness fastened. William Willard was too heavy for Harriet to shove into his seat, and he could not regain his footing.

She had to save William Willard! She did not want him to fall to his death. She knew the hazards to herself, but she had to help her passenger. Like the captain of a ship, she felt responsible for those who were with her.

Quickly, she unfastened her safety harness. Perhaps she could push him back into his place. Mr. Willard's body lunged forward. He was now pressing Harriet against the controls of the airplane. The airplane was speeding off course and out of control. The Bleriot monoplane rapidly plunged toward the water, and Harriet could not free herself from the weight against her to change its direction.

The pressure of William Willard's body against hers began to lessen. The danger to William was still present because now he began to slip from the airplane. Harriet grabbed Willard's coat and tried to haul him back inside the Bleriot monoplane, but he was too heavy. She pulled with all her might, but William's weight and the force of gravity were too much for her slender arms. She felt his clothing begin to slip from her grip. All the while the airplane continued to dive at a frightening speed.

She could hold him no more. She felt William Willard wrenched from her grasp. Harriet screamed as he fell.

A gasp rose from the crowd of onlookers below. They saw Willard's body tumble toward the water. A woman, transfixed by the sight, screamed in horror. A college student looked away. A father covered the eyes of his young son. One man crossed himself. There was nothing anyone could do as William Willard fell toward Dorchester Bay. His arms were outstretched as he seemed to reach for something to stop his fall. There was nothing for him to grasp. He plunged into the dark waters.

The force of gravity continued to tug at Harriet and the open airplane. She tried to gain control of the Bleriot monoplane, but it was too late. She could not change the course of flight of the small craft or hold herself in the airplane any longer. Gravity pulled them both toward the earth.

Harriet felt herself ripped from the Bleriot monoplane. A blast of cool air brushed against her face. It seemed quiet now. The airplane was flying away from her.

Harriet's eyes opened wide in fear. She saw the bay waiting beneath her. She knew the cold water would swallow her and that her brief life would end.

She had risked her own life for her passenger. She had not abandoned her airplane. She had proved herself as a captain and a pilot! She had done her job well. The water was closer now. . .

CHAPTER ONE

A NEW ADVENTURE

The Quimby household was astir although the hour was early. William and Ursula Quimby were busy packing some last minute household items and a few articles of clothing from the night before. Thirteen-year-old Kittie was helping them as they worked. Eight-year-old Harriet, however, was nowhere in sight. Perhaps she was gathering some herbs before leaving or climbing her favorite tree for the last time.

This was the day that the Quimby family had talked about and contemplated for so long. As a family, they had at last reached an important decision. They would move from Bear Lake, Michigan, to Arroyo Grande, California! The Quimbys were going to exchange the cold winters of the mitten-shaped state for the milder climate of the Golden State. William Quimby would leave his life as a farmer and would begin a new career.

It was not the first move for William Quimby and Ursula Cook Quimby. The two twenty-five-year-olds had come to Michigan in 1859 from New York State. They had been eager to begin a life together. The two had married at Ovid, Michigan, on October 9, 1859, and had settled near Coldwater, Michigan. They had chosen this area because William's mother lived here.

In 1861 a little girl was born to the pair. They named their first daughter Jennie. In the same year William Quimby left his wife Ursula and the farm house in Michigan to help the Union Army in the Civil War. Neither Ursula nor William knew if he would ever return safely to the Michigan farm.

William served as a cook for the army in blue. He survived the combat, the disease, and the weather. He was even able to visit his wife on several occasions, and a little boy was born to them on June 27, 1863. The proud parents named the child Willie L. Quimby.

At the end of the Civil War, William learned that veterans might apply for free land to compensate them in part for their services during the Civil War. This seemed like a windfall to the Quimbys since they were tenant farmers and owned no land of their own. William Quimby applied for a land grant from the United States Government in 1867.

The year 1867 brought both pain and pleasure to the Quimby family. A beautiful little girl Kate was born to the family on July 26, 1867, but just a few months later—on October 6, 1867—little Willie died of dysentery. The family was devastated.

On January 13, 1868, William officially received his 160 acres of land from the government. He signed for this tract which was about 200 miles northwest of Coldwater, Michigan. The area was in Arcadia Township in Michigan. Local residents called it "Bear Lake." William, Ursula, Jennie, and Kate packed their possessions and their dreams and moved to the new area.

Unfortunately, the family's unhappiness and misfortune had not ended. Little Jennie Quimby was not a healthy child and she took her poor health with her. Her cough and her weakness concerned her family.

Little Kate's sudden illness in 1868 compounded the grief and anxiety of the family. Her flu-like symptoms increased, and on August 2, 1868, Kate died of the "bloody flux." The family had lost two of its three children, and Jennie was still not in the best of health. Ursula was beside herself, and William grieved deeply for his children.

William attempted to make a living at farming, and Ursula resigned herself to the hardships in her life. The couple wanted more children, but Ursula was afraid for their health. She began to find out all she could about medicines, roots, herbs, and ways to keep her neighbors and family healthy and well.

Ursula and William had another chance for a large family! In 1870 Helen, a lovely little girl whom they called Kittie, was born to them. On May 11, 1875, another beautiful girl named Harriet—called "Hattie" by her parents—was born to the Quimbys.

Despite the best care that the family could arrange, Jennie died in 1878 of tuberculosis. The girls missed their older sister who loved them, watched them, and played with them.

Ursula, by this time, was the local expert on herbs, remedies, and other health preparations. She prepared medicines and sold them to her neighbors. In 1880 the family of

The William Quimby family homestead and most probable birthplace of Harriet Quimby—Located approximately three miles south of Arcadia, Michigan.

four moved to Manistee, Michigan, to try farming and selling their products in a different place. **The Manistee Times**, a local newspaper, contained an advertisement on July 21, 1881, for "Quimby's Liver Invigorator." A user of the product claimed, ". . .this valuable medicine is working wonders wherever it is tried, it will keep your system braced against disease by keeping the liver in good condition." Perhaps Ursula's knowledge of medicines worked especially well with Harriet ("Hattie") because she was healthy, intelligent, and hard-working.

The Quimbys anticipated no difficulty for Kittie and Hattie in the California schools. Both girls were doing well in the public schools of Michigan and in helping their mother with her medicine business. Even William Quimby sometimes helped to sell the products from the back of a wagon.

It was a good thing that the Quimby family had the medicines as an additional source of income because William was becoming disillusioned with farm life. William had placed a mortgage on their land in Michigan. He had been able to pay off the mortgage and regain the title debt free. There was now a second mortgage on the land.

They had packed to move. This time their travels would take them across the states to the Pacific Coast. Arroyo Grande, California, was waiting for them!

William and Ursula Quimby wanted this move to be their last. They hoped that success, health, and happiness would smile on them and their girls in this new land.

Ursula Quimby called loudly again for Harriet, her younger daughter. Ursula felt that moving days were hard enough without having to keep up with the vibrant eight-year-old tomboy!

However, when Ursula's beautiful daughter came running at her call, Ursula had to smile. Harriet's enthusiasm for life, her quick mind, her sparkling blue eyes, and her agility were appealing to all those about her. Truly, the Quimbys had an ideal family. Ursula's daughters always brought her happiness. Even in the busiest of times, their bright smiles, willing hands, and intelligent eyes warmed her heart.

Now the family of four was ready for a new adventure—one which Ursula hoped would serve to warm her heart as her family already did.

CHAPTER TWO

LIFE IN CALIFORNIA

Arroyo Grande, California, is about 175 miles north of Los Angeles. It was here that the Quimbys settled. William established a small country merchandise store, which he tried to fill with all the items his neighbors would need to buy. William liked the idea of one-stop shopping!

With his family to help stock the shelves and make the sales, William felt good about their future. He believed that the Golden State of California did indeed hold golden promises for the Quimbys! Perhaps the Quimbys could soon pay the mortgage they had left behind in Michigan. Maybe they could even put aside some funds for the future.

However, all the high hopes of the Quimby family did not materialize. Bad times again caught up with the Quimbys even in Arroyo Grande, California. Their general store did not succeed.

Returning to their farm in Michigan was out of the question. When the Quimbys had been unable to pay off their mortgage, the bank had sold their land at public auction in June of 1889. The family decided a new location would help them to get on their feet again.

The family packed their belongings and moved to San Francisco. Ursula decided that this time she would help manage the family's destiny and reestablish her medicine business. Seventeen-year-old Kittie had married in 1887. By the 1890s Harriet had finished school. It was Harriet, then, who was able to help her parents most with the work of their medicine business. The family enterprise began to prosper.

Ursula wanted to enhance the background of her family to the new neighbors in San Francisco. She spread the rumor that Harriet and Kittie had received their education in Europe. She said that theirs was a wealthy farming family in California. These exaggerations were part of a December 1911 article in **The Overland Magazine**. William Quimby, the fantasy continued, was at one time a member of the United States Consulate Service. **Overland** reported that Harriet had spent her childhood in France and received her education from private tutors.

Harriet was indeed a nontraditional young woman. In the late 1800s most women married, left home, and reared a family. Few women pursued careers. Harriet was quite different from the young women about her. She was staying at home to help with the family business. Although she was intelligent, social, and very attractive (traits usually associated at this time with those women who married), Harriet was planning no marriage in the near future.

Harriet was a "marriageable" woman, but she had made a conscious decision not to marry early. She had decided to pursue a career. Harriet wanted a vocation in which she could excel and one in which she would find enjoyment. Because she had been a good student with a talent for writing and because she enjoyed composing, journalism seemed the perfect field for her.

Ursula and William were not overjoyed with their daughter's decision. Harriet, however, was now a young woman who was old enough to make her own decisions. In truth, her parents were not surprised that Harriet was going her own way. She had always been intelligent and independent.

Harriet's first job was as a staff writer for the **San Francisco Dramatic Review**. Her second position was as a reporter for **The CALL—Bulletin and Chronicle**. Harriet was one of the best reporters on the California coast. She continued to play the role of a well-bred young woman with a European education. Harriet with her dark hair, her intelligent blue eyes, and her tall, slim frame turned heads when she passed. Her quick wit captivated those with whom she talked. Her articles were a favorite among the readers of **The CALL**.

In 1902 Harriet made some important decisions for her career. She would move to New York City and leave her family behind. She decided her work would come first and that the establishment of a home and family would come later in her life.

(NASM A44401A)

Probably Harriet's best photograph, taken in 1902 while she was living at home with her parents in San Francisco.

CHAPTER THREE

FREELANCING IN NEW YORK CITY

Harriet liked to say that she arrived at the "foot of Twenty-third Street" in New York City. Her description indicated that she arrived at the bottom of the business district of New York City. So far as she knew, there was not a single person in the entire city whom she had ever seen before. She was on her own!

Harriet found that jobs were scarce and that the competition was keen. At one point, things were so bad for the young woman that she even thought of abandoning her journalism plans and of working as a cook or window washer. Her money began to run low, but she managed to keep a positive outlook. She learned to view the competition as an incentive and not as an obstacle.

Harriet was bound to succeed. She had some letters of introduction, but she never used them. She possessed good health and a sense of humor, exhibited a keen intelligence, and made a good first impression. She was serious about her work and her seriousness came through when she talked with others. Still she could not find a job.

With her determination and creativity, however, Harriet found a way to advance her career. She became a freelance writer. Freelancing meant that Harriet was not an employee of one particular paper or one magazine. Instead she wrote articles and submitted them to newspapers and magazines which seemed likely to publish her materials.

Harriet found ideas for her articles in everything she did. She visited the Chinese settlement of New York and, being familiar with the Chinese quarter of San Francisco, found the area to be rich in ideas for articles. She enjoyed the scenes, the rich color of the area, and the uniqueness of the inhabitants. She based her writings on actual experiences. Harriet would not have dreamed of "faking" the facts. Truthfulness was necessary to her and to her writing.

Harriet generally had to find her own subjects for her articles. Occasionally an editor would approach her with an idea or a need of a particular newspaper or magazine, but the rule was for her to use her own sources. Harriet suggested that other prospective freelancers could get ideas for articles by talking with their grocer, a maid, or a waitress in the cafe.

Harriet had found a $30 story in a conversation with a maid who told of summer guests, duties, pleasures, and tips. A fruit dealer had talked about the purchase of grapefruit, and she produced a story which brought a sizable sum to her purse. Observing a customer purchasing pasta led Harriet to research the manufacture of the Italian foodstuffs. The result of her investigation provided a story and a tidy sum to help with her living expenses. Harriet's inquiry into some charities resulted in several columns—and several checks.

Freelancing proved to be a successful route to earning a living and to advancing her opportunities for employment. To improve her chances for publication, Harriet read all the magazines and newspapers she could purchase at the local newsstands or locate at the New York Public Library. These articles gave Harriet ideas on how to write, what particular magazines and papers published, and clues on items which were worthy of further investigation. For instance, Harriet read of a school which was opening to train washerwomen. She was there the next day and wrote a story which she sold for a tidy sum.

Harriet found she must live in a boarding house. Her financial resources were not such that other facilities were available to her. To avoid the gloomy atmosphere of breakfasting with strangers, to permit her time to read the morning papers uninterrupted, and to save pennies, Harriet found it more cheerful, more convenient, and less expensive to rent a room with a small gas-burner. She began to make friends and found several people with whom she could occasionally share a meal. Harriet particularly enjoyed the company of those who would rejoice with her over her sales and ignore her failures; she, in turn, gave them similar courtesy.

In 1903 when Harriet was 28-years-old (19 according to her mother), Harriet saw her first article in print in **Leslie's Weekly**, a magazine with many photographs. Harriet became a regular contributor to the magazine, which was one of her favorites. In 1904 Eleanor Frank, a reporter for **Leslie's**, went on a world tour for the magazine. Frank's assignment was to record experiences on this tour and use them in future articles for the magazine. Harriet filled in for Eleanor Frank on a temporary basis. By the end of 1905, Harriet had proved her value to **Leslie's** and had become a full-time writer for the prestigious magazine. In the fall of 1906 she became the magazine's drama critic. Harriet had launched an exciting, successful career in New York City!

CHAPTER FOUR

LIFE IN NEW YORK CITY

Harriet now lived a fairy-tale existence. Gone were the boarding houses, rooms with gas-burners, solitary meals, and concern about pennies. Harriet's home was a suite in the Hotel Victoria on Broadway—not a boarding house in an inexpensive district. Producers, directors, and performers made certain that Harriet was in attendance at opening night and that she came to the after-curtain dinners and receptions. They provided her with complimentary tickets and invitations to ensure her presence. They reasoned if Harriet attended, she might write about it and **Leslie's Weekly** might publish the review. The public read Harriet's articles. Hopefully, these reviews would be favorable and might increase ticket sales. The theater companies knew, however, that Harriet would be honest. They wanted to be at their best when Harriet was present!

Harriet not only sat in the best seats in the theater, but she could also bring her own companion. After the performance, she and her guest were often invited to the parties, late dinners, and celebrations of the performers, directors, and producers. Harriet met the most popular people in the city, sat with the most glamorous personalities, and dined with the stars.

Harriet's company was not an ordeal for the socially elite. New York society enjoyed her presence. The most eligible bachelors found her a good conversationalist and an attractive addition to the social events. Women did not feel threatened by her attendance. They knew that Harriet was devoted to her career. Because Harriet did not want to marry soon, women did not view her as a rival but as a friend.

After her free night on the town with her guest, Harriet would go to her office. She did not have to be there at the break of day. Her editor knew the long hours she spent gathering information for her column. He knew also that Harriet was dependable and conscientious. Her writings would be punctual, well-written, and accurate. By the end of 1906 Harriet had written over 100 articles for **Leslie's**.

Although Harriet found life in New York stimulating and her career rewarding, she did not forget her family. When she felt she was able to support her aging parents, she invited them to come to live with her in New York. Her mother came, but for some reason her father did not. He chose instead to settle in Greenville, Michigan.

Harriet became fascinated with speed and danger as early as 1903. She wrote an article for **Leslie's Weekly** on trick automobiling. In 1905 she wrote of the society woman's latest fad: the motor car.

In the fall of 1906 Harriet persuaded Herbert Lytle, a race car driver, to take her with him on a thrilling ride. At one point in the ride, the car reached a speed of 100 miles per hour—quite a pace for a car at that time. Harriet shared the event with her readers on October 4. During the ride, Harriet lost her hat. A photographer captured the moment for the subscribers of **Leslie's Weekly**.

Harriet had decided that motoring was for her. She applied for and received a driver's license. In the entire City of New York, Harriet was one of the first women—if not the first woman—to receive such a license.

Harriet's articles in **Leslie's Weekly** continued to reflect her interest in the automobile. For instance, in May of 1909 she provided some helpful hints for those who motored abroad. In 1910 she wrote on how one could use the automobile to save vacation money. A special article in January of

(A.E. Dunn)

Harriet after her exciting race car ride of over 100 miles per hour in which she lost her hat.

1911 informed the public about "Women Automobile Enthusiasts." Harriet's columns become popular and covered a variety of topics.

Leslie's included a wide breadth of subjects. By 1909 there had been over 100 articles on aviation and flight in **Leslie's**. One can imagine that Harriet read these articles with enthusiasm and studied the photographs with excitement.

Harriet also had become very interested in a particular pilot—the handsome John Moisant. Harriet followed his career in aviation and hoped to meet him someday.

The perceptive editor of **Leslie's Weekly** recognized Harriet's interest in flight and requested that she write an article for the public about the "perfect flying machine"—the American buzzard. The Wright brothers had used this creature of nature as a model for their airplanes. The Japanese, according to Harriet, were studying the bird as a way to help them solve some aeronautical problems with their own airplanes. Harriet enjoyed the work and asked **Leslie's** for more writing assignments about airplanes and flying.

The first air meet in the United States was in 1910 in Los Angeles, California. Harriet asked to attend and **Leslie's** encouraged her to go for reporting purposes. This meeting increased Harriet's enthusiasm about flying.

NASM (1910)

Poster advertising the Belmont Air Meet of 1910.

In October of 1910 Harriet covered a meet in Belmont Park, Hempstead, Long Island. Fifty thousand people came to observe the great race. The winner would receive a prize of $10,000. The course would be to and from the Statue of Liberty.

Most people believed a Frenchman by the name of Count de Lesseps would win. The winner, however, was the American John Moisant, Harriet's hero!

Harriet was very excited. She decided immediately to meet this dashing pilot and to learn to fly! She and his sister Matilde had their photograph made together at the meet and Harriet confided in Matilde her intention of learning to fly.

"I can do that!" she exclaimed to Matilde and her other friends. "It looks quite easy!"

Before the month was out, Harriet met the man she admired—John Moisant! She was thrilled! She asked him immediately to teach her to fly.

He responded, "Sure—I'll teach you how to fly—come on out to my flying field someday."

Some of Harriet's friends were not sure that she would really pursue her interest. They thought it might be just a passing phase. These friends did not know Harriet very well. Harriet was determined she would learn to fly!

Alas, her teacher was not to be John Moisant. On the last day of the year, Moisant died in an air crash. John's brother Albert, however, decided to continue John's work. He kept open the flight training school and the flight training operation.

Harriet believed that aviation would continue to grow. She wanted to keep the general public informed. She also wanted to satisfy her own curiosity about flying. She read and studied.

Harriet was well aware of the dangers in flying. By the spring of 1911 over one hundred people had died in aircraft accidents. More would die in the days to come. Harriet, however, could not forget her wish to fly.

In early April, Harriet went to the editor of **Leslie's Weekly** with her plan. Harriet suggested that she should become a pilot and report on her experiences in her articles in **Leslie's Weekly**. Her editor would not at first agree. Harriet was persistent. At last Harriet not only convinced her editor she should fly but also secured his promise to pay for her flying lessons!

(SI - A43515)

Matilde Moisant, John Moisant's sister, and Harriet at the Belmont Park Air Meet in October, 1910. Matilde became America's second woman licensed pilot following Harriet by two weeks.

The lessons cost $750. This was a great deal of money in 1911. Harriet was overjoyed! She could hardly wait to begin.

(Hayes & Co.)

Harriet Quimby dressed in her everyday work attire as a reporter for LESLIE'S ILLUSTRATED WEEKLY. "She was a pleasant, quiet and unassuming young woman, whom no one would suspect of being the most daring and famous air-woman of her time."

CHAPTER FIVE

FIRST LESSONS IN LEARNING TO FLY

Harriet read everything she could find about flying. The newspapers regularly contained historic events related to aviation. She exclaimed at the announcement of an air race from Paris to Madrid; the prize was $30,000. Harriet saw the tragic article about the pilot who flew into the crowd at the event and killed the French Minister of War. She grieved over the report of the German Zeppelin which crashed. She ad-

Members of the Moisant Aviation School with their instructor, Andre Houpert, at Hempstead Plains, Long Island, N.Y. Left to right, P.Wilcox, W. Kentner, M.F. Bates, A. Houpert, S.S. Jarvin, F.De Murias. Standing, Matilde Moisant and Harriet Quimby.

mired Glenn Curtiss and other pilots who set the standards. She dreamed of the day when she could break their records.

Harriet began flight training on May 1, 1911. She used the Moisant School of Aviation at Hempstead Plains, Long Island. Her personal friend Matilde, sister of the now deceased John Moisant, was also training for flight at the Moisant School.

Harriet could hardly wait to begin!

(American Press Association)

Harriet climbing into a Moisant Aviation School Bleriot for her first flying lesson.

Her personal instructor was Andre Houpert, the chief instructor pilot of the Moisant School. At the first lesson the instructor acquainted Harriet with the sound of the running engine. The instructor taught his student how to set the switch to prevent injuries when the engine started.

(American Press Association)

Andre Houpert, Harriet's flight instructor, explaining the operation of a Bleriot aircraft to her.

Four mechanics held the rudder until the engine reached the correct speed. At just the right time, they turned the rudder loose. The young pilot had to prove first that she could guide the airplane in a straight line for a mile or so. She had to steer the airplane successfully two times in this manner before the end of the first lesson.

(American Press Association)

Harriet preparing for one of her first solo flights.

At the next lesson Harriet had to guide the airplane in a straight line again—but this time off the ground. When she could control the direction of the airplane well, she learned to manipulate the wings of the airplane to keep it balanced. Lectures on safety and emergencies were also a part of the lessons. Confidence was an important part of the training. Harriet compared riding in the airplane to riding in a very fast automobile—minus the bumps, signals, and eyeing the speedometer.

(Aide)

Harriet's 1911 flight training class waiting for the fog to clear from the flying field at Hempstead Plains on Long Island during the early days of her flight instruction.

The local newspaper reporters interviewed Harriet about her flight lessons. Harriet told the reporters for the **New York Times** on May 10, 1911, that her plan was to become the first American woman to earn a pilot's license. She arrived on the field each morning at 4:00 a.m. to further her goal. Harriet shared her belief that flying was as safe as riding in an automobile. She viewed piloting a plane, however, as more fun than driving a car. Harriet ended the interview with the **Times** reporters with a question: "Why shouldn't we have some good women air pilots?"

The public was eager to find out more about Harriet's flight lessons. They did not have long to wait. The first of her articles appeared on May 25, 1911, in **Leslie's Weekly**. Harriet reported that she had been flying for two weeks. She was pleased that she was the first woman in the world to fly a monoplane, which had one wing on either side of the cockpit. The women pilots in other countries had flown biplanes, which had two wings: one above the other.

Harriet described her flying attire. There could be no flapping skirts to catch in the wires near the driver's seat. The pilot's legs and feet had to be free to steer the airplane. The long, traditional skirt was not appropriate. Harriet wore a suit of satin. The material had a wool backing, but there was no lining to the suit. She could tie the walking skirt to form pants. She covered the whole satin outfit with a coverall suit to prevent the castor oil which coated the engine from soiling her clothes.

Busy Harriet continued her flight lessons and wrote her articles for **Leslie's**. The articles contained information about the importance of air currents, aeronautics, and the danger of winds above 6 mph to flying. She described in detail the lesson in "grass cutting" (guiding the airplane in a straight line on the ground) and the more advanced practice of "kangarooing" (taking short jumps of two or three feet in height as the airplane rushed across the field).

The public was fascinated with Harriet. She received hundreds of letters requesting information about flying and many messages encouraging her in her efforts. **Leslie's Weekly** advertised an 11" x 14" poster of Harriet. The poster—together with a catalog of other available prints—was available for 25 cents. In the poster Harriet stands beside the Bleriot monoplane in her stylish flight suit.

Crowds flocked to air meets. An International Aviation Meet in Chicago brought 600,000 spectators. Accidents took the lives of two pilots during the event. **Leslie's Weekly** covered the events in its August 24, 1911, issue. The public was fascinated with flying!

(Courtesy of The International Women's Air and Space Museum)

Harriet Quimby – America's First Lady of the Air.

CHAPTER SIX

EARNING A PILOT'S LICENSE!

An important article in **Leslie's** was Harriet's report of earning her aviator's license, the first pilot's license granted to a woman in the United States. In fact, Harriet held the second pilot's license granted to a woman in the entire world!

Harriet officially had begun her studies in May of 1911; by August 1, 1911, she had passed the required tests. Harriet had taken a total of 33 lessons, each one lasting from two to five minutes—the same time stipulated in the schools of aviation in France.

At Harriet's lesson on July 31, 1911, her instructor Andre Houpert had told her that she was to try for her license the next morning at 5:00 a.m. Harriet had had no idea her examination date would be so soon. Nevertheless, she was willing to try. She was in bed by 8:30 p.m., but she did not sleep well.

The next morning long before 5:00 a.m. her telephone rang. Houpert told her that the fog was too thick for a flight. He advised her not to come until he sent a car to pick her up. The eagerness of Harriet and selected members of the Aero Club of America—which had to approve her flight—was such that they took a surrey through a fog so thick that they "could cut it with a knife."

Upon arrival at the field, Harriet found that visibility was indeed limited. A thick blanket of fog enveloped the take-off area. Her instructor was insistent that she wait. At

6:30 a.m. the field was clear, the sun was shining, and the monoplane was ready for flight.

Harriet later reported that her thoughts during the flight were more on the engine than anything else. She knew that if it failed, she would have to glide down—something she had never done.

Harriet described in detail in her articles the rigid tests she passed to earn the pilot's license. The International Aeronautical Federation on October 28, 1910, had set new rules. The new standards required an organization to award the license in its own country and to be a part of the international federation. The Aero Club of America was the approved organization in America. Harriet had to meet the new standards and work through the Aero Club.

There were rules to determine who could apply for the license. The applicant—who had to be at least 18 years of age—had to pass two distance tests. The airplane could not touch the ground in a closed circuit of not less than 3.107 miles. Each candidate had to fly an uninterrupted series of five figure-eights. Each successful prospective pilot also had to take the airplane to an altitude of at least 50 meters (164 feet) and stop the motor not later than the time when the airplane touched the ground. When landing, the candidate had to stop successfully within 165 feet of a point set before the flight. A fully-licensed candidate, finally, signed three completed forms.

A difficult part of the test for Harriet was to turn to the right during the figure-eights. Because she was right-handed, it was easier for Harriet to turn to the left. The test required the pilot to circle to the right and to the left for five consecutive times. Harriet landed with her face covered with castor oil from the coating on the engine. She was told she had not met the standards for the figure-eights.

Undismayed, Harriet said she would try again. She would wait for the engine to cool and then complete the second series of figure eights. She remained calm during the wait period and stuck with her plan to be the first licensed woman pilot in America! The next time Harriet tried the figure-eights, she performed to the satisfaction of her examiners.

Upon completion of this hurdle, Harriet began her altitude test. This flight began at 7:45 a.m. and ended six minutes later. Her friends and well-wishers were elated—as was Harriet! She had completed her goal. She had passed! She was the first American woman to have earned a pilot's license!

A newspaper reporter interviewed Harriet. Harriet welcomed the interview! She informed the writer that she looked forward to sitting back and reading about herself for a change. Harriet thought that others would pardon her for this pride.

(Aide)

Miss Harriet Quimby, landing in triumph after having successfully passed the Aero Club of America's flight test for her pilot's license. The date was August 1, 1911.

Harriet had already begun setting records. She was the first woman in the world to have qualified for a license under the 1911 rules for a monoplane. According to the Aero

Club of America, Harriet's landing was the "most accurate. . . ever made in America on a monoplane under official supervision." Harriet had become a pace setter already!

(Marceau 1911)

Miss Harriet Quimby, LESLIE'S dramatic critic and editor of the woman's page. This formal portrait was taken in 1911 soon after she gained fame as America's first licensed woman pilot.

CHAPTER SEVEN

A YEAR OF ACHIEVEMENT

Two days after receiving her license, Harriet performed by moonlight on Staten Island for 20,000 people.

Harriet could not have looked better. She walked with assurance and greeted her fans. They looked at her violet-blue eyes, her flawless skin, and her athlete's body. She was beautiful and confident in her violet satin skirt, high-laced boots, hood, and long-sleeved blouse. The audience saw her suit for the first time, and they loved her! The thrill of flying, the cheers of the crowd, and the joy of the moment made Harriet know she could never give up flying!

Harriet's mother, Ursula Quimby, greeted her daughter with a kiss after the night exhibition. She told Harriet that she would have come up for her if she had stayed in the air a moment more. Harriet replied that the feeling of flight was so great she did not feel like ever landing again.

In 1910 Alfred Moisant and his now-deceased brother had formed The Moisant International Aviators, an exhibition team composed of aviators. The team members asked Harriet to join their group. They would give exhibitions across the country and promote the Moisant airplane.

Harriet was delighted and gave her assent. By the end of September, Harriet had already won a cross-country race and $600, flown in the Richmond County Fair, and thrilled a crowd of 15,000 with a night flight for which she received $1,500.

(Brown Brothers)

One of Harriet's first flights as an exhibition flyer, early fall 1911.

Harriet was to remain with **Leslie's** for almost ten years. During that time she would see 250 of her articles in print in the weekly magazine. Harriet wrote about a variety of topics including travel, aviation, cultures, women's topics, food preparation, and investigative reporting. The public loved her writing and the subjects she chose. They accepted the fact that she was also a pilot.

The New York City Commissioner of Police, however, did not welcome one of her articles. She revealed some of his crimes, and he lost his job. Harriet continued to enjoy her work, but there was a new love competing with her writing: flying.

Her public eagerly awaited Harriet's articles. They even welcomed the columns in which she gave advice. Harriet often cautioned pilots and the public about the hazards of aviation. She warned others how to avoid the dangers in flight. She urged promoters of meets to ensure that the airfields were safe for the pilots and not to forget the value of human life. Harriet encouraged the aviators always to put safety first. She advised against reckless flying, overconfidence, and neglect in inspecting the flight mechanisms. She reminded her readers that between 1908 and 1912 there had been 109 aviation fatalities. She challenged those connected with flying to stop the accidents.

SAFETY DEVICE FOR FLYERS.
Twombly contrivance for preventing an aviator from falling out of seat or being crushed against the wheel. The device may be released instantly by the wearer.

(LEV. CK)

The type of pilot restraint device that was in use in 1912. Harriet was an advocate of safety devices for aircraft. This appeared in her last magazine article for LESLIE'S two weeks prior to her death.

Harriet advocated the use of harness restraints for the pilot and passengers.

Harriet's article about the dangers of flying and how to avoid those accidents was a milestone. She actually was suggesting the development of pilot check lists. Today a pilot has a set ritual of checks. This forward-looking woman proposed these preventative measures more than 75 years ago.

In October she and the Moisant group performed at the inauguration ceremonies for President Francisco Madero. Harriet became the first woman to pilot an aircraft over Mexico. It was a thrilling flight!

At 150 feet of altitude, Harriet's engine failed! Harriet had to make an emergency landing. That glide required Harriet's best skill as a pilot. Harriet, of course, landed successfully and later wrote about her flight.

During this period in her career, Harriet was still writing articles for **Leslie's** and working to achieve another goal: to become the first woman to fly the English Channel. Both Harriet's plans for flying the Channel and her work at

An early autographed photograph of Harriet.

Leslie's prospered. In fact, the editor of **Leslie's** instituted a new department devoted to the subject of aviation. Harriet became **Leslie's** new Aviation Editor.

Harriet was still living with her mother, but she was spending much of her life in the high society circles of New York City. Several young men were attempting to make Harriet a part of their life. Her agent Leo Stevens, for example, was a very good friend and was very fond of Harriet. Harriet, however, was not interested in marrying anyone immediately.

Harriet had been very fond of John Moisant. His untimely death in December 1910 was a great shock to her. Harriet still grieved for him and for the resulting loss to aviation. One way she coped with her loss was to throw herself into her work and her future plans: namely a flight across the English Channel.

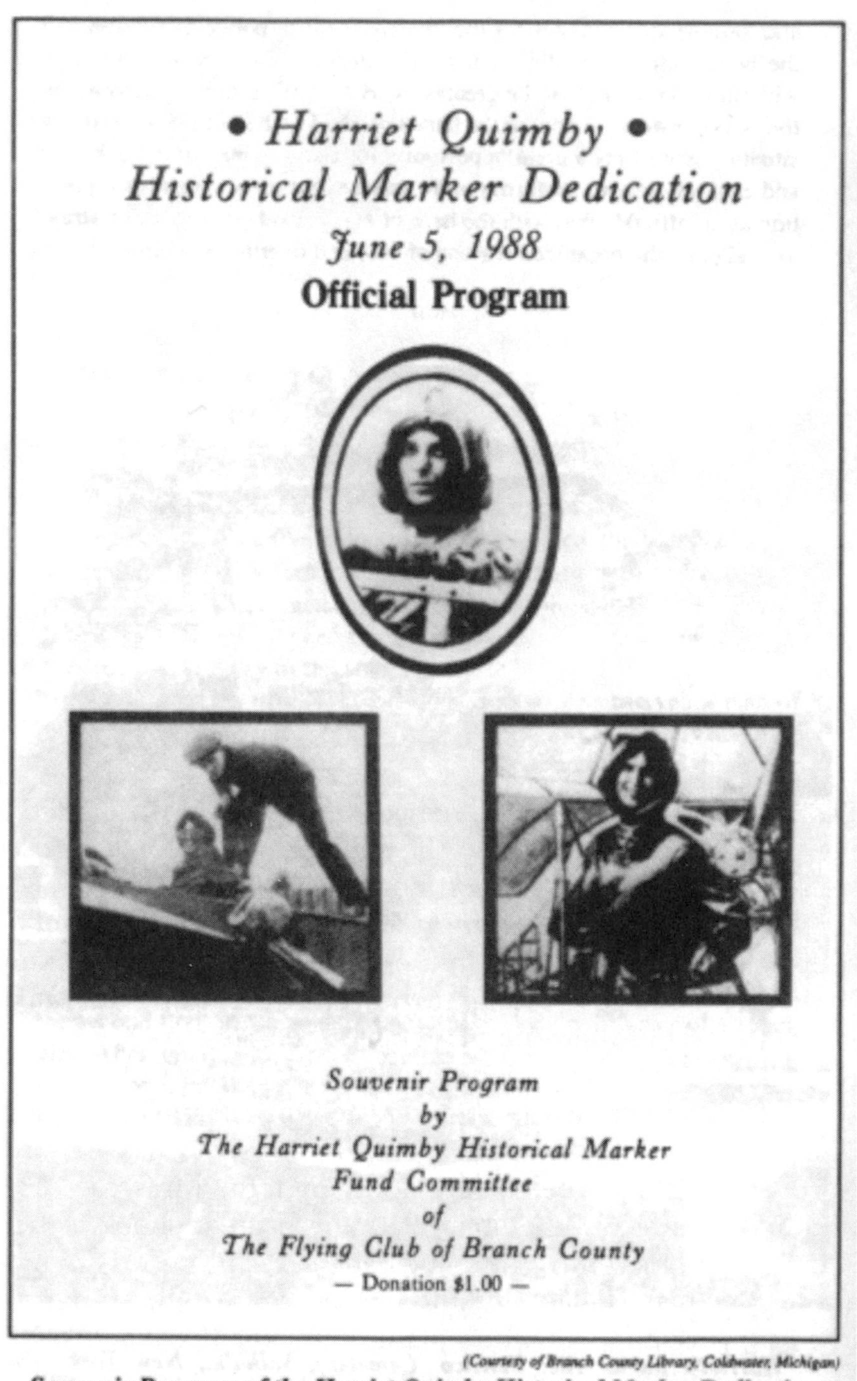
• Harriet Quimby •
Historical Marker Dedication
June 5, 1988
Official Program

Souvenir Program
by
The Harriet Quimby Historical Marker
Fund Committee
of
The Flying Club of Branch County
— Donation $1.00 —

(Courtesy of Branch County Library, Coldwater, Michigan)

Souvenir Program of the Harriet Quimby Historical Marker Dedication.

CHAPTER EIGHT

FLYING THE CHANNEL

The spring of 1912 brought new interest in flying. Engines were better. Airplanes were improved. Business was beginning to find new uses for airplanes. Harriet Quimby had become a role model for men and women. Men were saying, "If a woman can fly, so can I." Women were saying, "If women can fly, they can do anything."

(NASM)

Harriet Quimby posing for photographers at an early air meet in 1912.

Harriet began to plan in earnest for her flight across the English Channel. Her agent and business manager Leo Stevens agreed to help her. Harriet planned to contact Louis Bleriot, to buy one of his airplanes, and to make the flight in mid-April.

Harriet began to make final arrangements. She sailed for England in March. She gave the **London Daily Mirror** rights to her story and secured a loan from a London businessman for $5,000 to help cover her flight.

Harriet visited Louis Bleriot himself in Paris and ordered a Bleriot monoplane airplane from him. He shipped a Bleriot also to Hardelot, France, for her to try before the flight across the Channel.

Harriet went to Hardelot to try the airplane. She had heard of an excellent hotel in Hardelot and took a tramcar to the resort area. Harriet had underestimated her travel time by tram and arrived in Hardelot after dark. She was expecting to find a warm hotel waiting for her. She looked at the darkened building in horror! No light was shining a welcome to her. The resort hotel was open only in the summer! Harriet was in a strange town on a cold night with no place to stay.

Harriet went to a cafe that took boarders. There was no vacancy. She tried another place and rented the last space. The small room was cold and damp. There was no fire. The floor had no carpet. The pillow was small. The covers on the bed were stiff. But Harriet had a roof over her head and was safe in a strange country.

When Harriet went downstairs to eat, the maid asked for her autograph. Harriet asked her why she wanted her signature. The maid answered that she had heard Harriet was going to fly from Hardelot to England. Harriet signed the paper for her but asked that the maid—and several other people who were there—not tell the secret.

Harriet was eager to test the new Bleriot monoplane, but she found a gale wind of forty miles an hour blowing the next morning. All day she eagerly waited for the wind to die down so she could try out the new airplane. When the wind continued to blow, Harriet knew that she would not be able to try out the Bleriot monoplane.

Harriet inspected the monument erected to Bleriot who had flown the English Channel in 1909. He had flown from Calais, France, to Dover, England. Harriet reasoned that the White Cliffs of Dover were higher than those of Calais. She decided to fly the 22 miles by leaving from Dover and arriving in Calais—the exact opposite route from the one that Bleriot had used.

A trip across the English Channel by boat took about an hour. Harriet was not a sailor, but she looked forward to making the trip in a monoplane. She felt sure her trip by airplane would be a good one.

The next morning—Sunday—at 5:00 a.m. a gale wind was still blowing. At noon, however, Mr. and Mrs. J. Robinson Whiteley and their daughter invited Harriet into their home to lunch with them. Harriet welcomed the change because the gale persisted. Harriet was not flying though time was!

Harriet arranged to have the Bleriot monoplane shipped to Dover Heights about three miles from the English Channel. She was thrilled with what she saw at Dover when she arrived. Smooth sand shone in the spring sunlight. Its fine texture would allow for a smooth take-off.

Harriet was not the only one on the smooth sands. The Gaumont Cinematograph Company of London and the MIRROR reporters were patiently waiting for the flight. Harriet, too, looked forward to the take-off.

The famous Dover Castle pointed the way clearly to Calais, France, across the English Channel. Harriet decided that all she had to do was fix her eyes on the castle, fly directly over it, and speed directly across the English Channel to France.

The flight was to prove much more difficult, however. Harriet would be flying in very thick fog. She would be using a compass and an airplane, neither of which she had ever tried. If she drifted even five miles off course, the North Sea was ready to claim her thin form. Harriet, however, was confident in her ability to make the crossing. Her only fear was that someone would make the flight first.

Sunday morning, April 14, 1912, dawned a beautiful day—perfect for flying. There was one problem: Harriet would not fly. She had promised her mother she would observe Sunday as a day of rest, and no one could talk her into breaking her word to her mother—even though the weather was perfect.

The night of April 14, the early morning of April 15, and the day of April 16 were to bring tragedy to the world. Just before midnight on April 14, 1912, the great ship **Titanic** was on its first voyage to England. It struck an iceberg. The noble ship sank a few hours later, and 1600 people died in the cold sea.

Monday, April 15, 1912, was rainy and windy. Harriet could not fly in the weather, but she was eager to see what Tuesday would bring.

Harriet arose at 4:00 a.m. on Tuesday morning, April 16, 1912. An automobile took Harriet, registered as Miss Craig to avoid recognition, to the take-off point. Harriet determined she would fly this day no matter what the weather.

(LESLIE'S ILLUSTRATED WEEKLY/LONDON DAILY MIRROR)

Harriet Quimby and her party arriving at the Dover, England, airfield just prior to her English Channel flight.

The pilot D. Leslie Allen was also preparing for flight on Tuesday, April 16. Allen, the English flyer, was attempting to fly a monoplane across the Irish Channel from London, England, to Dublin, Ireland. Allen, however, left the London airfield never to arrive at his destination. Allen and his aircraft seemed to have disappeared. The Irish Channel holds the secret of his disappearance to this day.

Harriet's friend Gustav Hamel took the monoplane for a short flight since the Bleriot was virtually untried. There appeared to be some minor problems in its handling, but Hamel pronounced the airplane ready for flight.

Gustav's next task was to teach Harriet how to use a compass. She would need this instrument in the fog.

(LESLIE'S ILLUSTRATED WEEKLY/LONDON DAILY MIRROR)

Gustav Hamel giving Harriet final instructions on how to use a compass just before taking off to fly the English Channel. It was a skill she would soon desperately need that early April morning in 1912.

"Be careful!" he warned. "If you get five miles off your route, you will be over the North Sea, and you know what that means!"

Harriet did indeed know what it meant. It meant she would probably die from the cold in the open cockpit, become helplessly lost, or meet her death in the cold waters of the North Sea.

Harriet planned to fly from Dover, on the English coast, to Calais, France. Harriet, however, could not see the French coast through the cold, rolling mist. Along with her wool-backed, satin flying suit, Harriet wore wool gloves, a rain coat, a wool coat, and a sealskin stole. At the last minute a friend tied a large hot water bottle around her waist.

(LESLIE'S ILLUSTRATED WEEKLY)

Harriet suiting up for the English Channel flight. Preparation included tying a hot water bottle to her stomach to help keep her warm in the open cockpit of her Bleriot monoplane.

It was time to begin! Harriet entered the cockpit and began the final preparations. She was careful, of course, to fasten her pilot restraints.

(Brown Brothers/London Daily Mirror)

Harriet preparing for her early morning take off from Dover – April 16, 1912. Notice her necklace and "good luck" charm.

Harriet received her final instructions.

(SI-A31991F)

Take off time! Destination France! Harriet receiving final instructions just prior to her flight across the English Channel.

At 5:35 a.m., Tuesday, April 16, 1912, Harriet Quimby started her flight across the English Channel.

(LESLIES'S ILLUSTRATED WEEKLY/LONDON DAILY MIRROR)

The start of the Channel flight – 5:35 a.m., Tuesday, April 16, 1912.

In the air, Harriet soon found that mist covered her goggles. She could not see through the beads and had to push the glasses up on her forehead. She was traveling at an incredible speed: sixty miles per hour. She could not locate Calais at 2,000 feet. She dropped her altitude to 1,000 feet. Still she could not get her bearings. She dropped her altitude to 500 feet. Still she was unable to pinpoint her location. She was lost!

Harriet found that the wind was rising, and wind currents were gusting about the Bleriot monoplane. She decided that it was time to land. She looked below. All she could see were the plowed fields belonging to the farmers. Even at a risk to her own life, Harriet refused to ruin their hard work, their fields, their livelihood. She made a decision: she would land on the sandy, hard beach she could see below.

Harriet made an easy landing. She jumped from the Bleriot and stood on the beach. Where was she? Had she crossed onto French soil? Was she still in England?

The damp air was very cold. Her hot water bag was now ice cold! Harriet was alone on the beach. She did not remain alone for long. Soon joining her was a crowd. Children, men, women had heard the throb of the engine and had seen the bird light on the beach. They rushed to see what had landed. The people were speaking French! At last Harriet knew that she had succeeded! She had achieved something no woman had ever done: she had flown an aircraft across the English Channel!

The short trip had turned out to be much longer. Harriet had flown off course! She had traveled almost twenty-five miles out of her way, but she was close to Calais—her original destination.

Fortunately, this error had not placed her into the cold North Sea. Instead she landed at Hardelot, France. She was a few miles from her planned landing site, but she had reached her goal! She had made the crossing! Harriet Quimby was the first woman to pilot a monoplane across the English Channel!

(Brown Brothers/London Daily Mirror)

Harriet soon after her arrival on the sandy shore of Hardelot, France, 25 miles south of Calais.

The flight was one of many firsts for Harriet. It was her first time to fly by a compass, to pilot the Bleriot monoplane, to fly an aircraft across the water, and to fly on the other side of the Atlantic. She had achieved her goal! She had claimed a place in history for women everywhere!

CHAPTER NINE

AMERICA'S DARLING

The French crowd who gathered with Harriet knew what had happened! They knew that a woman had flown the English Channel and was sitting on their beach! They congratulated each other on the fame that had come to each of them. This woman had made history on their beach!

(Courtesy Tourist Department Hardelot, France)

A view to the south from Equihen overlooking Harriet's landing area.

Tucked between her coat and her clothing Harriet found a copy of the MIRROR. A friend had stuck this paper in Harriet's hand to use for added warmth during the flight. Now Harriet had a new use for it. She wrote a telegram on its margin in hopes a kind person would take the message for her to the nearest telegraph office.

Harriet was afraid to leave her airplane to send her own telegram. Although the people were helpful in every way, like a ship's captain, Harriet stayed with her Bleriot monoplane.

A young boy took the penciled message to a telegrapher. Later, a man on the beach placed a call for her. Neither deed cost her any money. Such hospitality was heart-warming to a cold pilot without any French money!

Those who gathered on the beach with Harriet began to try to make her understand that they had to move the airplane to higher ground. Harriet knew the monoplane would be a difficult object to move, but she need not have feared for her craft. The crowd handled the airplane with respect as they carried, pushed, and pulled it to safer ground. Even the children carefully helped with the move.

(LESLIES'S ILLUSTRATED WEEKLY/LONDON DAILY MIRROR)

Fishermen of Hardelot rolling the heavy Bleriot monoplane two miles to the Bleriot hanger located just inland from the small fishing village.

Harriet's actual landing location as reported in the LONDON DAILY MIRROR 18 April 1912.

(Courtesy Tourist Department Hardelot, France)

A view of the beach at low tide north of Hardelot with Equihen three miles away on the bluff.

(LESLIE'S ILLUSTRATED WEEKLY/LONDON DAILY MIRROR)

Harriet holding a tea cup presented to her by the people of Hardelot to commemorate her flight across the English Channel. The cup became one of her most prized possessions.

A woman gave Harriet some bread and cheese and a cup of tea. The warm liquid was delicious to the cold, tired pilot. The cup was a beautiful antique. When Harriet conveyed the message that the cup—six times the size of a normal cup—was a lovely one, the woman gave it to her. Harriet treasured the gift. She reported later in Leslie's that she prized no trophy more than the teacup a stranger gave her on the French shore the day of her successful Channel flight!

In the crowd that rushed to the site were Miss Whiteley and Miss Frances Drake, Whiteley's friend from Chicago. Harriet had shared lunch with Miss Whiteley on her earlier trip to France. In triumph, the two women lifted Harriet to their shoulders and carried her about the beach. Reporters and photographers captured the scene of two women celebrating another woman's achievement and

(Brown Bros./LONDON DAILY MIRROR)

Harriet's warm welcome to France after her epic flight across the English Channel.

shared the event with the world. Harriet reported that the fanfare made her very uncomfortable.

Later, Mrs. Whiteley served tea and cakes in the dining room of her mansion to the exhausted pilot. Harriet enjoyed the refreshment greatly! She traveled by automobile to Calais—a distance of about thirty miles—and then took a train to Paris. She had been awake for more than 15 hours! Tired but happy, she arrived in Paris, France, by 7:00 p.m.

Harriet triumphantly returned to the United States on May 12, but there was no reception for her. Competition with the **Titanic**, disapproval from suffragists who did not think Harriet gave them enough support, and the rejection of those who believed women belonged at home resulted in a lack of recognition both for Harriet and for her accomplishments. There was not even a "Welcome Home Parade" for Harriet from the city.

Everyone was not so unappreciative. Harriet continued her job at **Leslie's**. In addition to her job as journalist, she made many public speeches and appearances. She sometimes received a salary of $1000 for one presentation. Events, however, did not completely develop the way that Harriet would have liked.

In June, Harriet composed her last article for **Leslie's**. Through her article, her readers sensed her enthusiasm for flying. They, in turn, felt their own interest in aviation kindled by this foremost author on aviation.

The day before her departure for Boston where she was to participate in an aviation meet at Squantum Field, Harriet completed an article for **Good Housekeeping**. This article did not see print until September—after Harriet's untimely death.

(Hays, Detroit)

Miss Harriet Quimby, in a photograph taken shortly after gaining world-wide fame as the first woman aviator to fly across the English Channel.

CHAPTER TEN

THE END OF A DREAM

During the last week in June of 1912, Harriet arrived in Boston. She planned to break the speed record set in 1910 by Claude Grahame-White on his round-trip flight from Harvard Field to the Boston Light House. Harriet would have to replicate Claude's twenty-mile flight course at a faster speed to achieve her goal. During the late afternoon of July 1 Harriet decided to make a trial flight across Dorchester Bay.

Neither Mr. William Willard, the manager of the aviation meet, nor his son had ever flown before. Harriet offered a ride to one of them in the two-seater monoplane. The two men flipped a coin, and William Willard won! Five thousand people witnessed the take-off—and the crash.

Among the witnesses was Blanche Stuart Scott, another female pilot. Blanche wanted to land her airplane as a sign of respect when she saw what had happened to Harriet Quimby and William Willard. The crush of people on the ground below, however, prevented Blanche's landing on the field for some time. Blanche was now the only remaining American woman aviator.

The injuries to the bodies of William Willard and Harriet Quimby were, of course, severe. Harriet's legs and back were broken; these injuries probably occurred when her body struck the shallow, five-foot water in the bay or when her body came in contact with the mud beneath the water.

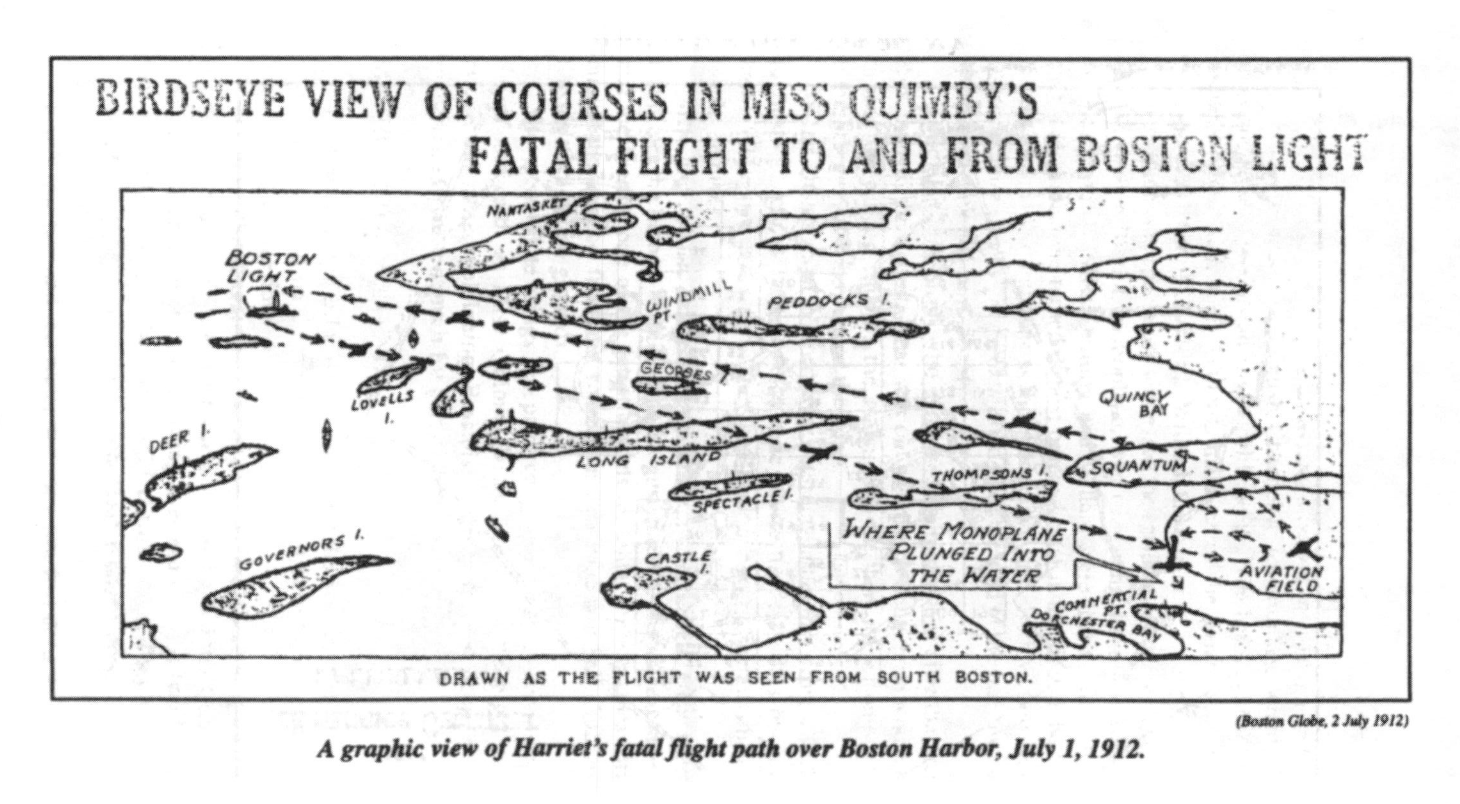

(Boston Globe, 2 July 1912)

A graphic view of Harriet's fatal flight path over Boston Harbor, July 1, 1912.

(LESLIE'S ILLUSTRATED WEEKLY/LONDON DAILY MIRROR)

Harriet beginning her last flight at Boston during the Boston Aviation Meet. Her flight was to have been a short speed trial run from Harvard Field to Boston Light and return. She was moments from death. The date was July 1, 1912. Flying with Harriet was W.A.P. Willard, a friend and the manager of the Boston Aviation Meet.

William, likewise, had a broken back and broken legs; in addition, he had suffered a fractured skull. Both had died instantly, according to the coroner, when they struck the water.

The Commonwealth of Massachusetts

STANDARD CERTIFICATE OF DEATH

PLACE OF DEATH

FULL NAME

RESIDENCE

PERSONAL AND STATISTICAL PARTICULARS

MEDICAL CERTIFICATE OF DEATH

I HEREBY CERTIFY that I have investigated the death of the deceased.

MEDICAL EXAMINER

(Courtesy Branch County Library, Coldwater, Michigan)

Harriet's Death Certificate. Note the California birthplace and age errors. Harriet was actually born in Michigan and was 37 years of age when she was killed.

These two deaths in July of 1912 brought the total number of fatalities in airplane accidents since 1906 to 154; forty-three persons had died in the year 1912 alone.

Harriet's parents took the first train to Boston when they heard what had happened. They were grieving when they arrived at the funeral parlor in Quincy. To make matters worse, somcone had stolen Harriet's famous satin flight suit.

When Harriet began her last flight, she was wearing her Aztec necklace. When her body was ready for burial, however, the jewelry was no longer in place. Harriet had lost it in the accident or someone had taken it from her after her death.

Harriet had just discussed the clay figure on the chain with a reporter from **The Boston Globe** the afternoon of her death. She had explained to the reporter that she was wearing around her neck a clay head created by an Aztec. The sculpture was about 2000 years old. Harriet wore the pendant on a silver chain from Mexico.

Among the Aztecs, artists made clay heads modeled after their kings; these sculptures replaced the photographs of today. Harriet smiled and said perhaps the necklace would bring her luck.

Before the clay head, Harriet often wore a brass necklace from East India—also thousands of years old—during her flights. Someone had mailed the brass necklace to a newspaper office in England for burning or melting because the owner wrote that the necklace "no longer worked." Harriet asked for the charm. Many people tried to tell Harriet that the necklace might bring bad luck, but Harriet wore it on many flights. When she began to experience some woes in her life, she laughingly told a friend that the little figure on the necklace may work better without a head. She used a circular saw to behead the little doll. Harriet believed people made their own luck.

Superstitious readers began to question if cutting the head off the brass idol had caused Harriet's death. Others wondered if Harriet had lost the Aztec clay figure and if the lack of a talisman had caused the crash. Most people, however, saw no connection between the crash and a clay trinket or a brass figure.

Memorial services for Harriet Quimby were in the funeral parlors of Frank E. Campbell at West Twenty-third Street in New York. Since the date of the service was July 4, the family scheduled the ceremony at 9:00 p.m. in order for many people to attend.

Present were Harriet's friends and members of three New York aviation societies: the Italian Aero Club, the Aero

Club of America, and the Aeronautical Society. Also in the congregation were many members of the staff of **Leslie's Weekly**.

The speaker for the memorial was The Reverend James B. Wasson of St. Thomas's Church. The Reverend Wasson reminded the group that through Harriet Quimby, people everywhere had been brought nearer to their goals.

Harriet's burial was on July 5, 1912, in Woodlawn Cemetery in New York City. At Harriet's special request the family used a burglar-proof vault. Harriet had asked her family before her death to purchase such a container. She had a fear that physicians might use her body for experiments.

Later her family decided to move her burial site. They had her remains exhumed on October 23, 1913. They reburied Harriet in the Kensico Cemetery in Valhalla, New York.

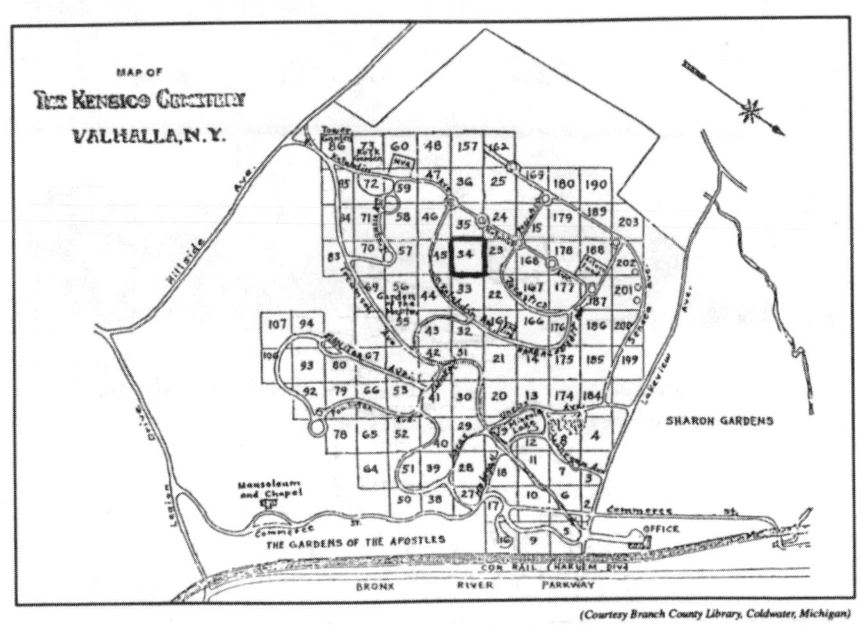

(Courtesy Branch County Library, Coldwater, Michigan)

Harriet's burial site – Valhalla, N.Y.

(Robert Ennis)

Harriet's burial site, Kensico Cemetery, Valhalla, New York. ***The plaque inscription may be read on page 63.***

Harriet had been one of a kind. Her flawless skin had looked like that of a Dresden doll. Young, beautiful, intelligent, talented, inquisitive, innovative, and perceptive, Harriet had peered into the future of flight in the world. Had Harriet Quimby lived out her life, she would have led the way in flight. Her good relations with the media, her personal fame, her popularity, and her connections with some of the most wealthy families in America might have helped

Harriet forge ahead into many new aviation areas long before others accomplished the deeds.

Harriet was flying twenty years before Amelia Earhart. Had Harriet not crashed into Dorchester Bay, her name—not that of Amelia Earhart's—might have been the well-known name of a woman aviator.

If Harriet had lived, it might have been she who flew solo across the Atlantic and not Charles Lindbergh. She probably could have completed this feat sooner than he. Lindbergh had been only a child when Harriet flew the Channel, and he did not fly the Atlantic until 1927—16 years after Harriet crossed the Channel. Harriet most assuredly could have accomplished this feat within ten years (1921) of her Channel flight—a full six years before Lindbergh.

Leslie's Weekly reported that with Harriet's death came the extinction of a brilliant light in the literary firmament. With her demise came the postponement of the dreams of a nation. With her life, however, had come a glimpse of the future of aviation and of women everywhere.

Many people of the time recognized her accomplishments. Through public donations and subscriptions, her supporters were able to erect a marker in her honor. The inscription read:

HARRIET QUIMBY

The first woman in America to receive a pilot's license to fly. The first woman in the world to fly a monoplane alone across the English Channel April 16, 1912.

The life of the heroic girl went out when she fell with her passenger aeroplane at Boston July lst, 1912. She was Dramatic Editor of Leslie's Weekly.

REST GENTLE SPIRIT

(Ed. Y. Hall)

Harriet Quimby Historical Marker, Branch County Airport, Coldwater, Michigan.

Dr. Anita Price Davis is a professor at Converse College, a private college for women. She holds degrees from Appalachian State University and a doctorate from Duke University; she is a former elementary teacher.

Dr. Davis has co-authored ten books to help students prepare for tests like the SAT and the PSAT; she has also written study guides for *I Know Why the Caged Bird Sings, To Kill a Mockingbird,* and *Inferno*. All are available from Research and Education Associates in New Jersey. Davis' *The South in the Revolutionary War: A Fun and Learn Book* is available at National Parks.

Anita Davis and Ed. Hall have written a companion book about Harriet Quimby. You can make a parachute, construct weather instruments, and work crossword puzzles about Harriet when you order this activity book from Honoribus Press, PO Box 4872, Spartanburg, SC 29305.

Colonel Ed. Y. Hall is a retired U.S. Army officer, pilot, aviation historian, and author, co-author or editor of six books: *Valley of the Shadow, Flying With the Hell's Angels, Fated to Survive, The Search for MIAs. Harriet Quimby: America's First Lady of the Air,* and *Harriet Quimby: An Activity Book for Children*.

He was born in La Grange, Georgia, and moved with his family to Harlingen, Texas, as a child. He attended Texas A & M College where he was a member of the Cadet Corps and the Class of 1960, Ed began a career that included service in various assignments throughout the United States, Europe, and Asia.

In 1980 Ed retired to Spartansburg, SC, with his family and joined the administrative staff of Wofford College. Ed continues an interest in community service, flying, and aviation/military history. Colonel Hall has maintained an association with the military and serves as a volunteer General Staff Officer with South Carolina State Guard.